THE DURHAM LIGHT AND OTHER STORIES

A PERSONAL HISTORY OF HOMELESSNESS AND SCHIZOPHRENIA

I0117223

Andrew Voyce

Andrew Voyce

Published by
Chipmunkapublishing
PO Box 6872
Brentwood
Essex CM13 1ZT
United Kingdom

http://www.chipmunkapublishing.com

Chipmunkapublishing gratefully acknowledge the support of Arts Council England.

This publication has been supported by the National Schizophrenia Fellowship and MIND

Contents

Andrew Voyce

Introduction

I was first admitted to a psychiatric hospital, in East Sussex, in early 1975. I was sent there by a magistrates court. I had been living rough in my car for about six weeks that winter and had been filling up with petrol and driving off without paying. For the next five years I was in and out of that hospital. I was admitted several times, usually for periods of up to a year and by 1979 I had spent about three years as an in-patient. I was diagnosed as schizophrenic. Previous to my admission I had undergone several traumas which combined to produce the classic case of genetic predisposition together with precipitating event or events in the late teens or early twenties. The first trauma happened at the age of seventeen when I was still in the sixth form at school. I suffered a motorcycle accident and lost a leg. Secondly, I had gone to university at eighteen but had failed my Finals after having two years off. My parents had divorced during those two years and this had not only deprived me of my place at home but had also meant that I lost the ability to work in the family firm. Another major factor was that I had become involved heavily in the drug scene and had at one time given up everything for a few months to do nothing but smoke cannabis. After failing finals I tried unsuccessfully a few jobs and, having lost all sense of responsibility, felt no remorse about stealing petrol and was eventually caught. During my time under East Sussex, I frequently lived rough to escape the medication regime of regular injections of a cocktail of tranquilisers and sedatives. This usually meant giving up the job and place I was living at before being returned to the hospital. I attempted suicide on two occasions because of the effect of the injections.

Late in 1979 I went on a government training scheme and again managed to escape the injections and this time I was sent to hospital in Kent near to my mother's home under section of the 1959 Mental Health Act. The advantage of this was that I had the right of appeal for the first time. The tribunal did not release me from hospital but they did recommend that I begin an Open University degree. After another year in hospital I was released to a Richmond Fellowship hostel in London but was back on injections. I managed to get a job as a clerk in the City of London and with encouragement from the warden I bought a house in the cheapest area of London. I stayed in the job for about four years before being made redundant after a take-over. Buying my own house gave me the independence to again escape injections. By this time, however I was becoming psychotic again and after getting my OU degree at the end of 1985 things fell apart in such a way that I was to endure severe delusions until placed under section of the 1983 Mental Health Act in 1991. My house was repossessed on the first of April 1986 and after a period where I travelled to Europe without a home I became destitute, living on daily DSS benefits until my final sectioning, with the exception of about a year after I received the balance of the sale of my repossessed house, when my homelessness became self-financed.

Since being released from hospital in 1991 I have lived under the 1990 Community Care Act in Bexhill. I persuaded the last hospital to give me medication in tablet form. They tried to administer routine injections again but after I threatened to do property damage they left me on tablets. I have now been here for seven years and in that time I have taken an honours degree with the OU, I have passed at B grade an A Level in History and I am about to obtain a Master's degree.

It is a pity that I could not have obtained qualifications in my twenties and have had some kind of career instead of having to fight the effects of injections all those years. I am now 47 years old. I am not a Thatcherite but I thank God that at last the old county hospitals have been closed down. There will be no more years of incarceration for me. The cosy situation whereby highly unionised staff could do what they liked for administrative reasons with the full support of doctors and managers has now been thankfully consigned to the past. It is not only a pity that something was not done in collaboration with my original university, but I could also have helped the police to deal with major drug dealers I knew of in 1975, and I could have recovered some money which I lost in the family firm. These matters gave way to administrative expedience and the routine administration of what were for me obviously mind-bending injections.

However I do not want this piece to be about social matters outlined above. There is such a thing as psychosis and delusion no matter what the environmental factors. The following chapters describe various delusory beliefs I had during my last episode of mental illness. Previously, my episodes consisted of minor paranoia and belief systems which I considered to be not serious mental illness. However, the five years described here without any medication did result in a kaleidoscope of schizophrenia.

The Durham Light

It became apparent to me whilst I was homeless for five years that a tactical move had occurred involving the Durham Light. My primary context was of course the coming of the Soviets (the five homeless years were 1986-91). It was obvious that the British state had collapsed. I had no contact with any agency or arm of the British state except the DHSS where I obtained £4.77 a day no fixed abode (NFA) rate dole money. Previously, I had quite a lot of contact with the British state: - tax department, government offices, hospitals etc. - so it was obvious that the British state had collapsed. And as the Americans were patently leaving Britain, the only thing that could be happening was that the Soviets were coming. As soon as the last vestiges of Americanisation had left Britain, as soon as there was no possibility of argument, then we would thankfully become Sovietised. To my shame, my last inside support system had been American, but those five homeless years including three winters outside in the cold and snow would have purified me. I would be sort of like a rehabilitated person from one of the Siberian gulag camps where people (prisoners) slept out in snow drifts. I was becoming suitable for inclusion as a Soviet, for when they arrived. And then my days working for an American company in the City of London could be forgotten. I would also be rehabilitated from having a mortgage from an American bank. I had caught the last end of American attempts to push the Soviets back. And not only was the local branch of the American bank in the county town where I remained homeless closed down, but by chance there was a branch of my former employers' insurance business in town, and the signs were that it too would disappear. The Wimpy bar had closed down. An American franchise. Good. And the Sock Shop had closed. That was reported in the Times (which I read every day in the town library) as gaining most of its profits from its American branches, so it too was good that another sign of Americanisation was gone. I took great pleasure in photographing their closed places (although the Wimpy later opened as Burger King). It was my contribution towards making the place safe for the Soviets. If I photographed an empty building, as usual my photo would be registered at the developers, and the Soviet reviewers could ascertain if any changes or activity were taking place, including if the building was booby trapped or fitted with a nuclear device. So all was proceeding well on the major front, with the Americans going and the Soviets obviously keeping an eye on things and ready to arrive when there would be overwhelming acceptance of them.

So where does the Durham Light fit into this picture? It was something I had discovered and it was the prime context for local British conditions. The Soviets would want it documented and under control. I am not sure of the exact order of events, but in my own deliberations it became clear to me that a set of events amounted to a tactic. It was a belief in this tactic that formed the basis for most of my conscious efforts during those days. In my mind, the starting point was the 1960's, probably 1962. At that time, the Durham Light Regiment had been disbanded and National Service had been discontinued. I seemed to have got confirmation of this from books I had read in the reference sections of libraries. What had the Durham Light done when they had been disbanded? Obviously they wanted something to replace what they had lost : free accommodation, free food, and pay. So they had taken a decision to occupy British Universities which were being expanded in the 1960's. Universities would offer their old conditions: residence in Halls of Residence, food in Hall, and a student grant. My memories of the new University at Reading had borne this out. I had met several Northerners, all from the North East. I counted the general area of origin as being centred around Newcastle and Durham, but the area would spread to Yorkshire and Southern Scotland. I seemed to have found examples of Yorkshire and Scottish regiments amalgamating with the Durham Light. Those Durham students I had met at Reading were there for those things: free food and accommodation, and a grant. They had obviously been told what to do by those wise old men in pubs when they reached 18. I seemed to have read about Teddy Boy riots in Newcastle in 1962 :- protests about the end of the army support. But now they had it in the new Universities. I told some people about this. One was a patient I used to visit at Oakwood psychiatric hospital. I used to visit him in the cold evenings to warm up a bit, and in return I would always take a couple of tangerines or something. I also wrote to my girlfriend at Reading. She still lived there, and had married a student from - Yorkshire. To my eternal shame I wrote to her and told her that her husband was a Durham Light and that I was in the real world where I numbered Soviet dead in millions; - the Durham Light was nothing. That was something else about the Durham Light - they always went after our Southern women. I recalled all the student sub-culture groups I had known, and in each group the one who ended up living with a girl was never a local, a Southerner. It was always a Durham. I counted Manchester in with Durham, because it was a commercial, trading, centre out to get something for nothing, as had the Durham's. As far as I knew and thought, the Durham Light had no battle honours and therefore the Army for them had been something for nothing. Just like the Universities, something for nothing. But done on a deliberate, tactical basis.

Now, in the late 80's, the Durham Light had moved on. I lived in a world of ancient beings, and to become an ancient being it was necessary to be part of a strong military movement yet at the same time be very much personally dominant and perhaps willing to suffer and make sacrifices. The Durham Light had come to occupy police stations. They were becoming like ancient beings, only staying in police stations as long as they could stay awake. If you were ever in police cells, the officers who brought you tea, meals and cigarettes were never the same. No officer had permanent duties in police cells. So it was obvious that they were using police stations for personal shelters, probably to avoid being magically transferred to another world (which I fully believed in) where they might come under nuclear attack. By communicating with young beings they avoided the doom to which some beings who were hundreds of years old came to. And not only did they use police stations, they also used new police vehicles and petrol. This gave them little protective capsules to move between stations. They got their traditional benefits: free accommodation, food and pay. Just like in the Universities. Another step on for the Durham Light.

But in their roles as policemen, and there were some North-Easterners in Southern stations, the Durham Light were performing a role relevant to the Soviets. Our reality in Britain was centred around the Durham Light and what they were currently doing in pursuit of free food, accommodation and pay. They were acting to protect and advise Irish people in caravan sites, and to keep them from giving anything away about the IRA's purpose of getting just one man through to assassinate the Archbishop of Canterbury. It became apparent to me that I had never met an Irishman without meeting a Durham Light first. That was true at Reading University and elsewhere. There were no Irishmen in the police and none of the Irishmen at Reading had succeeded with Southern women, but they were looked after by Durham's. I concluded that the Irish lived on caravan sites and that that was the way they moved through the United Kingdom. Wherever they set up a site the police would leave them alone, except to make sure they were OK when it became impossible for them to stay. There had been historical immigration between Ireland and Southern Scotland, and that might have involved temporary accommodation including caravans. The Irish would be allowed in, but not to take permanent Scottish homes. Because of the Durham Light's links with Scottish regiments, the Irish immigrants would be sent into North East England. And as the Durham Light had gone national via the new Universities and now in police stations, so their protégées the Irish could be sent to where the Durham Light were. Which included police areas like the one where I was homeless. I photographed caravan sites to log if any homes changed. I thought I was documenting movements. I photographed sites I was convinced housed Irish people, of course protected by Durham Light policemen. My theory was borne out by several events. Once, as I was occupying the woods near to Oakwood hospital, I was appalled to see two children aged about ten and eight riding a motor-tricycle. There was some exchange of words and they had Irish accents. I concluded that they had come from the nearby temporary caravan site on which were subsequently built new wards for the expanding general hospital. I had photographed the caravans and this site had become a focus for me in logging developments in my Irish/Durham Light scheme of things. So, I had discovered Irish people on a temporary caravan site. And they had enough money to give their kids an expensive Honda tricycle. They wouldn't be moved on because the Durham's in the local police station didn't consider it time yet. There was a clear link between America and the IRA in the shape of Noraid, a fund raising organisation. And now they were spending their money in the heart of the South of England, threatening the Archbishop of Canterbury, their religious rival, and a key figure in what was left of the British state. The Soviets would not arrive to restore order for homeless people like myself until this American link via Noraid and the IRA had gone. On this particular caravan site I took action, over and above photographing. I got fallen branches from Barming woods and lit fires that burned long ways. I lit them at dusk and burned them into the early hours, but in the direction of the caravans. I don't know if I would have set fire to any caravans - I might have done because I sometimes did dangerous and stupid things. I considered this would be like a signal and a threat to the Irish in the caravans, and would confirm me as a Soviet fighter. But as soon as my fires got out of the woods and began to cross open ground towards the caravans (after a few consecutive nights lighting), the caravans moved. I considered this to be a victory, and something that would do the Archbishop some good, as the Soviets could come to terms with him.

Another incident with caravan sites confirmed my theory that the Irish lived there, and that they had become part of the American-financed Durham Light tactic. It happened thus: I was sheltering from some drizzle in a church gateway (I often sheltered in church gateways or bus shelters). A white Bedford Astravan drove up and an Irishman got out. After several tries, he persuaded me to go with him to work in tarmacing for "ten to fifteen pounds a day". He actually took me to a caravan site nearby at Sevenoaks, a town I knew well. The caravans were parked on an abandoned petrol station. As well as the Astravan, there was an oldish Mercedes and a newish Ford Granada. There were more Irishmen there. They were big and well dressed. The boss Irishman told me they had a contract for a £1000 tarmacing job that would take a day, and myself and another local waif on the site could do the work. I concluded that they were going to do an extortionately - priced job, probably for a local old lady. And pay us two £10 to £15 each. A woman on the site brought us a meal of potatoes and gravy, and I spent the night in a caravan that seemed to have a bed covered in lots of rags. I considered I had got valuable information on these Irish rip-off merchants who were obviously going to send money back to the IRA in Dublin from their extortionate profits. But I knew what to do. The next day, I left early and waited for the chemists to open. I bought a film and walked back to the site. There I stopped 100 yards from the site and photographed it in Morse code, with normal shots for dashes and vertically - held shots for dots. I also shouted out for the site to be taken. When I went past the site to photograph it from a bus a few days later, the caravans had gone. I considered this to be a victory on a par with the

Barming caravans. I had a great sense of personal power. My use of the camera and signalling had amounted to the use of a weapon. The fact that I was photographing in military fashion made my shots effective. Elsewhere in parallel worlds my equivalent would be armed differently but would be out, as I was, to destroy caravan sites because they represented the long arm of America via Noraid and the Irish people who I had proved lived there.

I found other evidence of a link between caravans and police stations. At the traffic police headquarters just outside the county town of Maidstone, there were a dozen or so old caravans parked behind the building. This was clear link between the caravans and their protectors in the police. The caravans and the HQ were visible from the train between Barming and Maidstone. So, for some time I used the train just so that I could photograph those caravans. Also, I can recall seeing a caravan parked outside a police house in Sevenoaks which was confirmation of the Durham Light/Irish caravan dweller link. I found further evidence that caravans were coming south.

One day, I resolved to make an investigative trip to Durham itself. I went up to London and took the Durham coach from Victoria coach station. As we went up the MI, I saw lorries taking large caravans south. They were flat- backed lorries with one caravan on the flat back and one being towed behind. I delightfully photographed them from the coach. When we reached Darlington, in the

Durham home area, I noticed a caravan depot. It was thus obvious that the Durham Light had a depot from which they were sending caravans south for their Irish friends, right in the Durham area. I missed the early evening coach back and took a coach to Leeds, hoping for a connection to London. There wasn't one, so I slept in a car park and got a coach back to London the next day, armed with evidence that I by now anticipated, that the Durham Light tactic was the major feature of reality in British society.

As for Irish efforts to get at the Archbishop of Canterbury, I discounted the Irish / Durham Light set up as the source from which the attack would come. The police and caravans were obviously a form of permanent settlement, not inoffensive, but not directed against the primate. No, his threat was to come from someone like me. Someone who lived in the countryside and who, unlike me, would have no link with officials at all. No dole because that would mean the record of a Giro. No means of support except the land. The food he could get from the footpaths he would be taking from an Irish port towards Canterbury. Nettles, grass etc. And in the summer, he would live off berries. So I conducted a campaign against this lone, unseen Irishman. I cut down blackberry bushes close to the footpath route from the countryside to Maidstone and then on to Canterbury. This would deny the unseen Irishman food. And then I met him. I had been collecting my dole and spending some of it on a Stanley knife to cut down blackberry bushes, and had been doing that for some months, when I flushed him out. I was in a Maidstone park when I got talking to a poor man who, it was clear, had, like me, an artificial leg. As soon as he opened his mouth I knew I had succeeded. He was Irish. He was thin and drained, obviously not well fed. So he had made it all this way from an Irish port via footpaths and then found no berries to live off. I immediately lit up a cigarette and began blowing long-short puffs in Morse code. I had succeeded.

Andrew Voyce

Active Service

Whilst I was wandering about and mostly homeless, my perception of life led me to believe that I was primarily engaged in some kind of military activity, on a self-funded and self-initiated basis. It was up to me to discern what the situation was and to then proceed on my own steam. I knew I was not capable of going out and shooting or bombing someone- that occurred in parallel worlds that I communicated with. My task was to observe and signal where possible, for the benefit of people in my own world and to influence my enemies and allies in parallel worlds. I had allied myself to the new winning side, the incoming Soviets. My connections with the American-dominated world had obviously not sustained me and I was preparing myself for a life over the future centuries where I could provide a complete universe for myself in the name of the Soviets. As well as having to perform military tasks, I had to behave in a manner compatible with political commissars. I had to be politically correct in Soviet terms and also do something useful for their military machine. I had not only to observe by photography and photocopying texts of what I had encountered, it was perfectly alright to do character assassinations and other publicity in connection with Soviet landmarks. This was what I had to find out about, including using local libraries.

There were some events that convinced me of the reality of military life. Once, I had settled down for the night in a churchyard near Maidstone when some people entered an adjoining field. There was the sound of gunfire and pellets went through the trees above me. They were probably shooting pigeons, but I thought that this was the effect of a real engagement in some parallel universe that had filtered through to mine, and I felt in real danger. I kept perfectly still while the firing was going on and was very careful about cover and crept away the next morning. For me, that was active service and I had been under fire.

Certain aspects of my signalling were also significant to me. I was convinced that two places where sets of four carparking posts were located meant that Morse code was in use as that had a maximum of four digits. One set of posts was opposite the Post Office next to the new shopping centre. I thought that people would signal Post Office details from the entrance to the Office where there always seemed to be people hanging around. It was obvious to me that these details would be passed from the door of the Post Office to the signalling point opposite from where they would reach unauthorised, probably American, hands. I therefore told a security guard at the shopping centre that this was going on. A few days later I noticed that one of the posts had been removed, and I thought that I had done some good by telling the security man who had then had the post removed, thus preventing the crucial four digits being signalled. This was useful active service.

On another occasion I had a real success for my methods. I was in the library looking up religious facts when I came across the five tenets of the Sikh religion. They were the five 'K's which included the turban and the knife. Feverishly, I put the book down and headed for the most prominent local 'K' I knew, which was bus stop K. There I saw a Sikh in a black turban getting out of a car. This was, I thought, perfect timing and highly significant. I got out a cigarette and blew a Morse code signal in triumph. This was for me proof of my own reality and true service.

My photography was a military asset. At times when I had money I would take a reel of film a day and have it one-hour developed, preferably at Kodak's in Maidstone. At the time, I knew of the Peace Women at Greenham Common, the so-called 'Smellies'. Had I gone there my camera might have been useful, for photos of military installations are very sensitive. I could have photographed Cruise missiles and American soldiers, but I kept to my 'home' area and used photographic sensitivity there. However, instead of having a chief Smelly to give my photos to, all I could do was to leave them at sensitive places like under the door of the Crown Court at night for my secret allies to collect and process. One particular fascination for me was a helicopter that was the forerunner of the air ambulance. I felt there was something wrong with the whole thing and photographed it many times, especially landing at the new Maidstone hospital. I left these photos lying around at the hospital bus stops and elsewhere as well as copies of Janes military aircraft profiles of the type of helicopter they used. I was determined to expose this helicopter and assist anyone who was also interested in it who used busses.

I also tried character assassination. My stepfather's insurance company had an advertising campaign on the side of busses I used, so I wrote and photocopied vitriol about the company and put in my stepfather's name, date of birth, telephone number and address so that any cranks could have a go at him. I left these articles around, but especially on busses which carried the adverts. I used to board them specially.

Another person I had a go at was my old university professor. I had looked him up in Who's Who in the library and he listed membership of the 'Conservative Homosexual Group' and the Reading branch of the Campaign for Homosexual Equality. I copied this entry and highlighted the homosexual references. I then sent them to all the women's Halls at Reading University. Later I wrote some vitriol against the professor and attached a copy of the Who's Who entry, suitably highlighted and regularly sent it to persons at the university, hoping to discredit him. The above were necessary and laudable acts of political warfare so I thought.

An incident occurred at Barming Station car park which for me highlighted the aspects of being under fire as much as when shotguns had been fired over my head that night in the churchyard. At the time I was very involved with infrastructure changes which were happening to my local environment. The main lane through Barming had been straightened and there was major construction work with the new district hospital. The work on the hospital had included the presence of mini-diggers at the old nurses home. I had photographed most of the changes so that it could be recorded that I now lived in this world. Perhaps one day I could create my own facsimile world or return to the old Barming where there was a twisting lane, for I believed that these places still existed in parallel worlds which one day I might enter. Then, one Sunday I was at the station car park waiting for the bus which was replacing the train that day. There were several mini-diggers at the far end of the car park. I had already photographed them. As I waited for the bus, a low loader entered the car park. What was it doing there on a Sunday? It was not an ally as it came from the company that had done much of the roadworks which were not in my interests. As the low loader came into the car park, I photographed it. The driver immediately turned towards me and actually struck me twice. Then the driver got out holding a lorry tyre iron. He threatened me with this and made me hand over the film. He also demanded to know what I was doing there and I said I was waiting for the bus. He then drove off down to the end of the car park where the diggers were. Fortunately the bus arrived and I left before anything else occurred. Instead of, say, complaining to the police in Maidstone it became just another homeless day. But I felt I had been in action and felt I had performed well. These people knew we were after them and knew whose side I was on.

In my capacity as urban activist, I had started campaigns just before leaving my Plumstead home due to repossession. I hated the traffic noise in Plumstead and identified large diesels as the prime cause of nuisance. I therefore decided to start a movement called the Plumstead Voluntary Association for the Reinstatement of Horsedrawn Dustcarts. I opened an account at the Woolwich building society and paid money in hoping that one day the account would prosper and the people would be able to buy horses and carts and a depot to replace the noisy diesel dustcarts. However this idea became redundant when I lost my house and started to live rough in Kent. Nevertheless, I found a purpose for the account when I was homeless. I paid in money at branches in the SouthEast from time to time because although the Woolwich had obviously not wanted the Association and had therefore contributed to my downfall through non-action, I now saw that an active account would cause them confusion. It was sort of reverse financial sabotage. After I had been admitted to hospital to end my period of homelessness, I was resettled to a residential home. I gradually forgot the tactic of financial sabotage although there were one or two incidents immediately after I was resettled. I found a soulmate in the home who had been in the T.A.

and we both agreed it was a good thing when I photographed a caravan site one day whilst passing on a Social Services outing. Also, we were both left alone once in a Social Services office where there were old papers and a photocopier. We seized the chance and copied everything in sight before leaving with the papers stuffed under our jumpers. Amongst our haul was a paying- in slip with the Social Services account number. So we paid in 50 pence to confuse the system, as I had done with the Plumstead Voluntary Association.

Active service for me meant self-taught low-level military-style and urban activities, and the reinforcement of my reality by actual minor events meant, for me, that I was becoming an effective agent for the incoming Soviets, who were obviously winning the Cold War and who would appear as soon as there was unanimous support for them.

Aerospatiale Ecureuil

I was concerned about all major changes in my environment that could have strategic implications for my world and for the incoming Soviets. This included traffic, air movements and overflights of my civilian area, building and road works, as well as the more overt military movements from the nearby barracks at Maidstone.

One new development concerned me for quite a long time. It was the introduction of the Kent Air Ambulance service. I was aware of publicity to raise funds for the air ambulance helicopter. When I was sleeping rough near to the new Maidstone District General Hospital I began to notice a helicopter landing in the grounds. What I managed to do in cases such as this was to analyse the specifics in the noisy busy area that I was in to find out exactly what was going on. I began by photographing the helicopter as it landed near the hospital. It was a plain helicopter, not marked with the red cross or any distinguishing marks. Some men dressed in boiler suits would get out and go into the hospital. They would not carry a stretcher. Then they would come out again and the helicopter would take off again with a tremendous noise. I began to get used to this routine and used my camera to record as much as possible. Sometimes I would move away from the hospital when the helicopter arrived and photograph it as it was gaining height. I soon got to recognise patterns in these movements. The helicopter would arrive at the same time each morning. It would always come from the south. It became obvious to me that this was no emergency service, rather it was a regular military-style routine. I studied my photographs which included one day when it flew dangerously close to the hospital building. I considered this to be a threat to the hospital. In Maidstone library I took out Janes aircraft manual and identified the helicopter as an Aerospatiale Ecureuil. The specifications of the Ecureuil were that it was built by the French company Aerospatiale in Europe and was also built under license in the US and in Brazil. It was intended as passenger transport or for military spotting purposes. There was a larger Aerospatiale helicopter which was intended for purposes including as an air ambulance. I would return to this book many times for further information and to photocopy the page on the Ecureuil so that I could leave information in significant places such as near the landing site or at the bus stops at the hospital.

In October 1990 I was arrested whilst passing through Hailsham and sent to the psychiatric wing of Eastbourne district general hospital for a month. I was confused because at that exact time the Soviet satellite of East Germany ceased to exist with reunification. I did not see it as the writing on the wall for the Soviet Union, rather I thought it was some convoluted way of telling us that our ways were in some way acceptable to the incoming Soviet forces who had somehow done a reverse takeover. I considered that what I was doing was still good. I still had to help prepare the way . Whilst in the hospital I discussed some of my night-time traffic photographs with a nurse whose husband was a policeman and this added credibility to what I was doing in my own mind. Then one day I noticed the helicopter flying in from over the Channel. Previously in Maidstone,I had looked at the range and speed of the Ecureuil and had also seen that the French had a helicopter carrier at Brest. I thought it likely that the Ecureuil was therefore being sent over each day by the French Foreign Legion. The fact that the helicopter was coming in over the Channel confirmed this. I therefore got my camera out and one day photographed it. The next day it was slightly later and somewhat to the East. The next day the same. For me that made three short movements, or three dots. The next day there was bound to be a big movement to signal a dash so as to make a total flying pattern of dot-dot-dot-dash, which I thought was the most powerful signal you could make. So I calculated where and when the next day this final movement would come and went down to meet it, and sure enough there it was. I photographed it gleefully, having caught the helicopter in the act. I thought also that my camera would have the effect of a radiation beam on the pilots, so helping me to aid the Soviets even though I was temporarily inside. This series of events was the most significant to me of all those around the Aerospatiale Ecureuil, but it continued to play a major part in my life and I continued to travel to places on its flight path to photograph it.

Andrew Voyce

Arthur Blue Van and Fieldings Mercedes.

At one point in my homeless life I received the change from the sale of my house in Plumstead which had been repossessed. It amounted to about £13,000. It was not enough to buy another house so I decided to live without benefits for as long as possible. I actually lasted about 15 months. I didn't get in anywhere but I was able to do a lot more than when I was on the dole. For example, I took a reel of film a day and had it one-hour processed. But the main change in my life was that I didn't have to be near the dole office in Maidstone to sign on every day. So I was able to travel and to spend time away from Maidstone because I was no longer tied to the dole office. One place I visited was Sevenoaks. I knew Sevenoaks quite well. My parents had used me as a builder's labourer in their building firm whilst I was at grammar school and I had helped to build two dozen or so luxury houses in the town. It was whilst I was on one visit to Sevenoaks that I ran into Michael, who I had known in a psychiatric hospital and also at a Spike (hostel). Michael let me stay a couple of nights at his caravan on a site in a valley a few miles from Sevenoaks town centre. There was a regular minibus from the bus station in Sevenoaks to the site, twice a day. However I fell out with Michael for several reasons. I had suggested to him that we could get the train to London. There, he could use one of my cameras at one point whilst I stood around the corner and we could photograph the traffic simultaneously to check that none was disappearing as it went around the corner. This I suspected was what was happening. But Michael started talking to some people while I was taking the money out of the Post Office for the day's trip and I strongly suspected them of being American agents. He also refused to walk in single file on the narrow pavements of Sevenoaks. So I photographed him and did not go up to London. Instead I concentrated on Michael's support system, which centered on the blue Transit van driven by a man called Arthur between Sevenoaks bus station and the caravan site which would otherwise take hours to reach from the nearest regular bus route.

Over the next few weeks I made a thorough job of reconnoitering the route of Arthur and his blue van. The weather was atrocious. It poured, and there was no shelter out in the countryside on the route to the caravan site. I gave my wax jacket, which I wore on top, a real test. Each time I wanted to photograph the blue van I had to get as near as possible via public transport and then walk through the country lanes or footpaths across fields to the vantage point where I wanted to photograph next. I photographed the blue van at every junction so that it was clear which way it went whenever a decision would have to be made about which way it had gone. I traced Arthur's route back to early morning before he picked up at the caravan site, and in particular I thought this was very important and breaking new ground in the surveillance of the blue van. As there was a trace of private enterprise about the minibus, it being not an official bus, I was especially concerned with the implications about it being American. I considered all the while that what I was doing was for the Soviets who had obviously got the upper hand in the Cold War and who would be buying copies of my photographs from the developers. I considered that I had got somewhere by photographing the phenomenon of Arthur Blue Van and that I had fulfilled a duty. The long walks into the country and the survival of the drenching rain had been worth it. I could eat a few expensive takeaways out of my £13,000 knowing I deserved them.

Also in Sevenoaks I was able to attempt further analysis of traffic. Traffic was a constant problem with no apparent pattern to its pervasiveness. I noticed some things, like every Astravan being white and every Fiesta XR2 of about 1989 being either red or white, but in general out of the vast amount of traffic on the roads of the south-east there was no common pattern. Except for Arthur Blue Van. And Fieldings Mercedes.

I noticed that in Sevenoaks, which is a very affluent commuter - stockbroker town, there were many special Mercedes cars. They were unusual for the day in that they were either coupes or two-tone. Such Mercedes I had only come across once before. That was in the City of London, where I had worked as a clerk. Those Mercedes belonged to a firm of insurance brokers called Fielding and Partners who were rapidly becoming very rich with a brand new building in the City where they parked their distinctive Mercedes cars, which were all coupes or two-tone in colour, very unusual. As these cars were now appearing in Sevenoaks, I concluded that there was some move by Fieldings into the town.

About the same time, I used to visit a village near Sevenoaks where the library had one of the few copies in Kent of "Operation Julie". This was a book about some drug dealers, one or two of whom I had known while a student in Reading. One of the dealers was called L**f Fielding and his claim to fame was that he could supply G.I. grass, sold to American soldiers in Vietnam and grown in Thailand. These Thai sticks were the strongest marijuana at the time. The book in the library evoked the presence of that whole group. Then, I noticed in the travel agents window near the station where I photographed the special Mercedes, adverts for a special holiday to Thailand. The whole picture fell into place. L**f Fielding was connected to Fielding and Partners. The London insurance brokers were gathering in Sevenoaks either to all go off to Thailand together with L**f and the other Operation Julie dealers, or else to wait for the dealers to fly off from the travel agents and return with supplies of Thai stick. I decided to publicise this activity and wrote the complete allegation down. I then took it to the photocopy shop in Sevenoaks which was, to my mind, where all local publishing took place, and would get ten or twenty copies, making some pointed and loud, triumphant remark like: "Nice day for a flight to Thailand!" That would be enough to register my story for the Soviets who would buy copies from the printers. I would then dump all my copies in some significant place, like the travel agents or for the local dustmen to find. It was well known that KGB men and MI5 men searched dustbins for evidence and information, so I would be letting them know and putting the fear of God into someone who would realise the implications of my exposé.

All in all, my time visiting Sevenoaks may have seemed to the man in the street like some tramp arriving in possession of a mad camera. But in logging Fieldings Mercedes and Arthur Blue Van, I was convinced that I was performing a very meaningful activity.

Doppelgangers, Signalling and Traffic Analysis

What is a doppelganger? A doppelganger is a double, a twin, and can have sinister overtones. I have come across doppelgangers in films and TV, in programmes like The Avengers and The Prisoner and I can recall one World War 2 film about Germans dressed in US uniforms, speaking perfect English who infiltrated Allied lines and then directed American soldiers towards Nazi tanks. There have been Avengers programmes about secret enemies coming ashore on lonely beaches and imitating local people before of course killing them off and taking over their lives. I came to believe that this was a common process and my first realisation made me quite paranoid. I was living in London and the lenders were threatening to repossess. At the same time something horribly coincidental happened. My full name is R.A.Voyce, quite an unusual name. However, when I got on the telephone for the first time, I discovered that there were two other R.A.Voyces in the telephone book. Together with the court proceedings to repossess my house, I came to the conclusion that someone was imitating me and that they were going to have my house. These other Voyces were possibly fictitious, and behind it all was someone in the High Court who had decided to get hold of my house by some devious means I did not understand, but it involved someone taking over everything in my name. This made me very frightened and aware of danger. When I went to the High Court, the official presiding, Master

Munroe, was obviously the character behind it all. I came to believe that he was probably very old, and may once have been a monarch, possibly James 1, who had over the years survived by using the skills he was good at, namely legal documents. In a way I was being selected to receive his venom and the force of the law. Later, when I had finally lost my house and become homeless, I no longer felt paranoid about this episode as the official had got what he wanted, my complete ID, and I could be safe but of course poor. This stealing of ID later became an obsession. My ID had always worked. In particular, my National Insurance number always got me benefits, and I assumed that it would be valuable because of this. When I was in spikes-DHSS resettlement hostels- I was constantly aware that the dispossessed men there had probably been replaced by doppelgangers who were living the good life on their ID's.

When I was in Sittingbourne spike, there was a character there who had definitely been my father at one time, and another who might have been. My father had been thin until the age of about 30, when he had put on a lot of weight and become an intimidating person. His personality had also changed, and when he was big he had been occasionally generous and mostly a bully. His putting on of weight had coincided with business success and wealth. I concluded that an incoherent man at the spike had been my father in his big and generous phase, but that the wealth had now been taken over by the ogre who was a

Stalinist infiltrator who had got hold of the ID. (Before he got rich my father had been a communist trade unionist.) The man at the spike could not talk properly and was unkempt with a beard and old overalls in which he used to clean the stairs every morning, but the physical resemblance and gentleness of character convinced me that he had been my father in his generous phase. He was obviously very old and probably connected to the spirit of the Russian Revolution, but he had been replaced by the tyrannical Stalinist who had taken over his ID, and who was now masquerading as a respectable middle-class Englishman. I believed one day that Sid in the spike would have a shave, a bath and a haircut and would put on a smart suit and return in his rightful place once someone got him his old ID and legal papers back. Another man at the spike might have been my father in his thin days, but I was not completely sure. He was called Geordie and had a fearsome shot at five-a-side football, but his general fitness and working-class credentials made me think that he might have been my father as a working man, and could be again, once someone got him his old ID back.

I believed that this doppelganger effect had to do with ancient beings who would use signalling as a kind of power or weapon and that by teaching myself Morse code I had somehow entered their world. Amongst the ancient beings were Sid and Geordie. However, I had taught myself a wrong Morse code, and although I thought I had learned it correctly at Woolwich library, my code was almost entirely wrong. I got the ones everyone knows right. SOS is dot-dot-dot dash-dash-dash dot-dot-dot. Therefore S is dot-dot-dot and O is dash-dash-dash. After that I got almost every letter wrong. For example, I thought A was dash-dot whereas in fact it is dot-dash. In my code, J and Y were the same, as I thought they never occur together in any words. But my signalling did not take place over wires. I believed Morse was everywhere. I believed birds sang in Morse and that trees and nature in Europe were arranged in Morse. I would decipher sounds and try to respond to them. When I was on remand for minor offences, I would listen to the jailer's keys and tap back in my Morse. I would listen to pop music and decipher it. In particular I remember the group U2 whose guitar sound is based on two notes, one high and one lower. This I interpreted as dots and dashes. I would listen in jail and tap back. My own version of Morse was with me everywhere but I did not know I had got it wrong. I quite happily went round with code with me wherever I went.

In particular, I believed that dot-dot-dot-dash stood for B and was short for "Back!" This was for me the most powerful signal and I used it constantly. I blew smoke in Back to protect me and the beings I was communicating with. I got small pots of paint and painted trees and fences in the country in Back. This was partly to protect the area with the power of dot-dot-dot-dash and partly to mark out the boundary. I slept rough in woods if it was fine and in summer houses in the old psychiatric hospital if it was wet. This area was Barming, on the edge of Maidstone where I got my dole. To the west was West Malling, an old World War 2 RAF area. I considered the RAF to have been in with the Americans whom I regarded as my enemies. Hence West Malling and everywhere westwards towards the USA itself was enemy territory and it would be good if the border which I patrolled could be marked out. So at night I would wander around the fields so no- one could see me and stop me performing this important strategic task. As well as Morse, I discerned other signs which I considered it important to observe. I had been in a hostel in the East End near the original Royal Mint. This had been developed by Henry 7. I thought he would probably be alive in some guise. Coincidentally, at around the astrological cusp of the month, I seemed to find old florins in my pocket (they used to be 10p pieces). I thought this was something to do with Henry 7, so on the cusp I would leave some florins at a prominent part of the nearest town. I thought that would be significant.

Also in the East End, I believed that ancient beings from the City of London would be about. I thought that workmen on a building site were probably from Roman times so in order to acknowledge them, every time I went to the cigarette shop I would walk in a pattern that marked a Roman sword as I walked. If you see a mentally ill person walking in a peculiar way, it may be for some similar reason.

I thought there was great signalling significance in numbers, especially money amounts. When I had money, I would use it to signal. For a Post Office account, in the late 80's the minimum deposit was £5. So I would deposit £5 and a number of pence to write a message. The pence would stand for letters of the alphabet, for example 1 would be A and 2 would be B. By depositing £5.04, £5.09 and £5.04 I would be spelling "did". Then I might spell out "paint" to signify that I had recently painted a Morse sign somewhere. I tried to read significance into the money sums I received, especially the numbers on Giros, again turning numbers into letters. However, my main signal was always Back. I can remember mowing the grass at Sittingbourne spike and using the throttle to sound dot-dot-dot-dash as I went along. The mower seemed to work better and of course I was doing something significant.

Traffic was always a focus for me. When I had my first psychiatric episode in 1974, I was living in a car and driving aimlessly. Whenever there was a crisis, such as when I was about to run out of money or even just get out of the car, I seemed to run into lots of traffic. This made me paranoid and I thought that traffic was somehow intercepting me, and that it was being directed towards me. By the time I was homeless and living rough as a pedestrian in the countryside between 1986 and 1991, I no longer had this paranoia about traffic, but it was the major influence on my life. You cannot walk along any country road in Kent or Sussex without meeting traffic, day or night. I decided that I needed to get to the bottom of this, and that systematic observation was necessary. When I could afford it, I would photograph traffic and look at the photos to try and see what traffic met me and where. Particularly at difficult times, such as on dangerous country bends, I would use my camera like a gun to capture the traffic and to drive it away. When I looked at the pictures afterwards, I tried to see if any cars were the same, but they never were. All I could do was to sort the hundreds of photos I had into categories such as red cars or blue cars. However I believed that my photographs would somehow be registered at the developers and the information might be bought by the Soviets and that they would find the information useful or else be able to identify and log the cars I had photographed. This would count as a useful purpose that I had served. As I had an obsession with signalling, I also believed that traffic would be doing some sort of signal to the Americans who obviously were in control of the UK traffic environment. When I could not afford to use my camera, I would nevertheless make an effort to analyse traffic. I would buy indelible pens and do traffic counts on lampposts wherever I was. I would mark the number of cars, lorries and motorcycles passing me over a few minutes and then aggregate the figure into a rate per hour and write it on the lamppost. Also, I would do the same exercise on pieces of paper and leave them to be found by dustmen who I believed would always sift through rubbish for messages. One particular category I found significant was "small noisy motorcycles", especially at night.

So my behaviour at that time would have been quite antisocial and embarrassing, but not really illegal. Wild attempts at photographing high-speed traffic, visiting the same Post Office several times a day to pay in small amounts, leaving rubbish about and tapping and banging my feet on busses and in cafes. Perhaps you can recognise that in someone you know.

Mesmerism, Stasis and Ancient Beings

My full-blown experience of mesmerism and stasis occurred in Hamburg, Germany. Prior to becoming homeless and destitute when I missed a signing-on day and had to make a new social security claim as a homeless person, I travelled frequently around Europe by spending my savings and redundancy money, by going into debt on credit cards, and chiefly by claiming mortgage payments from the DSS but spending the fortnightly Giro on cross-channel ferries and European trains. At that time I found that I could easily stay awake for four days and nights, and actually planned my activities around this. I would set off from England having cashed my Giro and would not expect to need a hotel or sleeping berth on a train for four nights.

One evening I arrived in Hamburg and made my way from the station to the docks district of St. Pauli, where there is the Reeperbahn and red light district. I spent the night in a bar talking to a German about St. Pauli FC and their next match. How I did it I don't know because all I know about St. Pauli is its geographical location; I know nothing about the football team. Also in the bar was an attractive young German woman. She was tall and blonde, and had an English Staffordshire Bull Terrier on a lead. She talked some time about being in California. This made me unsure, for although I was not penniless, I had been made redundant by an American firm and my home was the subject of possession proceedings from an American bank operating in the UK. But I was most uncertain of all about America because I had been turned down for a visa to visit America. My opinion of America was beginning to change. Well, after my night in the bar and the next day wandering around the city, I booked into a hotel and had a night's sleep. I woke the next morning and was walking towards the main station after breakfast when I happened to pass a jeweller's shop. There, motionless in front of the shop was a paralysed woman. She was elegant and in her thirties, and on the end of a lead was a Staffordshire Bull Terrier, like its mistress, also paralysed. They stood there, the woman staring at a clock. They were kind of shimmering, surrounded by an ephemeral aura. I was amazed. What was this phenomenon? What would happen to the woman and dog? Just then, a woman emerged from the shop. She was small and old, and was wearing a Swiss-style cloak-coat and hat with feather. I stood there still in amazement when, quick as a flash, the old woman just touched the stasis-bound woman and walked on past me. The woman and dog awoke. They ceased to shimmer and the woman turned in surprise to look at me and left the shop window area.

This had a profound effect upon me. I had been privileged to be introduced to an astounding natural force for a few seconds before the old Swiss lady emerged to stop it. But what did it mean? Were the woman and her dog mesmerised by time itself in the shape of the clock? Time must be one of the most powerful elements known to humans. Had this powerful force overcome the woman and her dog? In those moments of mesmerisation, what had happened to her? Had she, from her point of view, been looking at a clock one moment, and the next moment had I just appeared in the jeweller's window? Was the old Swiss lady connected with the Swiss clocks and somehow associated with the purveyance of the power of Time? And what would have happened if the woman and dog had continued to shimmer? Would they have just gradually disappeared and then have been there, but not there at the same time? These considerations passed through my head almost immediately and remained with me for a long time. They became the basis of reality in a lonely and fragmented world. I became convinced that we could all be mesmerised by powerful and primeval forces and transferred into states of suspended animation before being re-awoken as the old Swiss lady had awoken the woman and dog in the jeweller's window. I became convinced also that there was a strong connection involving the dog. Staffordshire dogs are rare in Germany, so it seemed likely that the dog was the same one as had been with the young blonde in the bar in St. Pauli. Perhaps the person was also the same. It was merely that she had been in a young blonde woman in the bar, and in an elegant older body at the jeweller's. Perhaps she had already lived about ten years whilst I only experienced one night. Perhaps that is what happened when stasis and suspended animation occurred. I became deeply affected and began then to experience the power of ancient forces. Time was just one of them. There would also be forces like the power of the sea and the power of ancient and modern deadly weapons. In the same way that chickens swoon at the sight of the shape of a hawk being swung, so humans would swoon at the presence of powerful forces that have been around since time immemorial. And we would not awake until our eternal protectors emerged to save us from what would be a condition of suspended and perhaps invisible animation. The force that I grew familiar with was the force of signalling, and I came to believe that I had discovered the secret of the intrinsic power of the signal as obeyed by all of nature. This would become my own personal trademark in this world that I now perceived contained great forces that caused incredible effects on our bodies.

Some time later, financial disaster overtook me. I was late arriving back from Europe to sign on for my Giro which would have included an amount to pay the mortgage, and which I would usually spend on European train travel. Because I had cleared my house contents and could not substantiate a new claim including mortgage subsidy, and because there was a possession order on the home, I got into a hostel near the coast and made a DSS claim there. But the hostel evicted me, and I was left homeless, only being able to claim an amount for subsistence. It was not so bad as the weather was warm, and by that time, things like eating regularly and sleeping in a bed at night were not important.

I wandered along the coast at Folkestone. I had been thinking about mesmerism and how easy it would be to fool travellers on the sea. Most cross-Channel passengers, certainly those who were travellers for the first time, would not actually know what Dover looked like, or Calais, or any other channel port. Change a few signs and Vlissingen would be the same as Boulogne. So where were all these people going? It appeared to me that as there were lots of unoccupied areas on board all ferries, people in stasis were likely to be on board. I was travelling at the time of the Zeebrugge disaster, but it appeared to me that the controlled capsizing of ships going between anonymous ports might be routine, as a way of somehow affecting those people on board who were invisible and in suspended animation. It was just that in my limited world, together with the people I shared it with, these things were not reported or known. But things were in fact so advanced and on such a grand scale that to a person in control of the mesmerisims and fears of the sea, it was not a problem to capsize and then re-float a ship, perhaps many times. So most ordinary passengers could be put to sleep and they wouldn't know any difference when they arrived. They couldn't even recognise one port from another, let alone stretches of coastline or other features of the sea. All this had something to do with the struggle between the Americans and the

Russians. World War Three did not consist of nuclear bombs. It consisted of the playing of ancient and powerful forces. In my world the Americans had let me down. So the obvious conclusion was that the Russians were winning and would arrive soon. (The whole period of these episodes is about 1986-1991, near the end of the Cold War). But the Russians would be arriving in force by arriving in ethers. They would use their powers of telekinesis and thought control power and emerge as mesmerising beings. Now that I was like a Siberian prisoner, homeless, I could be rehabilitated from my American-financed ways.

So I was wandering one sunny morning down some long steps in a gardens at Folkestone when to my amazement a whole crowd of people suddenly started walking up the steps. I felt paranoid. Why was this happening to me? I braced myself and carried on. I walked down and along a promenade. It was a hot hazy day on the coast. My glasses had been broken some months before, so mid and far distance objects were not very clear to me. I was also wearing sunglasses. But as I walked, stopping regularly along the promenade by the beach, I looked back and forwards. Where I had looked before there seemed to be groups emerging from the haze and merging with the other people on the promenade. They appeared to be changing places. What was this? It was the same phenomenon of shimmering change-over from one world to another that I had witnessed in the jeweller's shop in Hamburg. But who were these people changing over? It came to me that they were people being exchanged between Russia and America. Probably in preparation for a final separation between their two worlds - capitalist and communist. The Russians were coming to our world via the media of ancient forces, and on this heat-hazed day, people were merely walking from one time lock to another, through this staging-post on the shores that appeared to be the English Channel. Then, as I reached the end of the promenade, I saw the symbol that was acting as a supernatural magnet for this process. There appeared to be a sand bank, and I recognised the silhouette of a World War Two battleship stuck on the bank. There were flashes of light nearby. I assumed that this warship was shelling. A powerful scenario, capable of evoking the most basic fears in anyone. A necessary requirement to enable a mesmeric trail to be laid between America and Russia, one along which people could move between the two disengaging enemies, whilst all parties not directly involved would go into suspended animation at the very hint that a World War Two battleship was about to open fire.

A few days previously, I had an experience that convinced me that along with the ancient forces went equally ancient beings who acted as guardians or controlled these forces. I was sitting in an ice-cream parlour in Folkestone when in walked five or six giants. They were all at least six feet six in height and had muscular 20-stone plus frames. They were all dressed in 300 or 400 year old military uniforms. I was convinced that they were as old as their uniforms, different colours like black and brown, with tricorn hats. I know now that such theatricals are part of some Kentish festivals, but at the time it seemed obvious to me that I was in the presence of ancient beings who could mesmerise everyone merely by drawing a sword or aiming a musket. I built up a world of similar ancient beings in subsequent months and years. I believed that Jesus lived. He just happened to be 2000 years old. I had read a short story by D. H. Lawrence called "The Man who Died" about the risen Jesus wandering off to become a healer in nearby villages. I believed this to be as true as the Bible, and evidence that the 2000 year old Jesus was somewhere in the domain, along with the 400 year old Marines I had seen in the ice-cream parlour. I believed that certain areas would be the province of a local ancient being. I believed that ancient Archbishops of Canterbury were now living as lower clergy under the present incumbent. I believed that there would be a surviving knight from the Battle of Hastings who I thought of as Norman Knight. I believed I came close to him sometimes if I went near Norman castles or churches.

One thing that these ancient beings would have in common was their control over ancient forces. The Germans have a word "Sel" which means force like magnetic attraction. I believed that these were attractions operating through the ethers of stasis whereby a being in one world could affect a parallel reality. This was my interpretation of "Sel". By doing something meaningful in my world, I could affect other worlds, and perhaps help the magical powers of the incoming Russian Soviets who were acknowledged to be masters of mysterious thought processes. I believed I had discovered an eternal truth in the power of the Morse code signal dot-dot-dot-dash. I knew there was Tchaikovsky's 1812 Overture which went dot-dot-dot-dash. However, in my learning of Morse I thought dot-dot-dot-dash was "B". I took this to be "B" for "Back". By signaling "B" you were saying: "Get Back". Pigeons and other birds did this. Once when I had a small radio I listened to a program about the Narvik battle in World War Two. In the program all the guns were shooting in Morse "B". (Actually Tchaikovsky was writing V for Victory, the true translation of dot-dot-dot-dash). So as far as I was concerned gunfire had to have a message to be effective. You must say "Back!" when you fire. And by signaling "B" in Morse in smoke when I had a cigarette, or by tapping on a coffee cup (for which I was barred from one cafe) or by painting trees or posts or buildings in the middle of the night, I would be doing an intrinsically powerful thing and I could advantage friendly beings in parallel worlds. It seemed to me that when I marked out the western (America-facing) boundary of my area with Morse signals on trees and fence posts, the trees actually began to point defensively westwards. If it could have that effect on trees, then perhaps the other elements in some minor but nevertheless significant way would be saying to Americans to stay away. This was my contribution to the progress of the incoming Soviets, who would make themselves known only when there was no opposition, and when the forces of nature were suitably set against their enemies. It was of course necessary to be ideologically sound, and we would have to order our world so as to accept the total victory of the strong Stalinist version of Communism. We would have to know the difference from Trotskyite International Socialism. Only by doing our bit towards setting nature against Stalin's enemies could we hope for salvation. Then the Soviets would arrive, and the mysteries of mesmerism, suspended animation, and ancient beings would lead us into a long and safe life.

The Political Context

My life seems to have mirrored or coincided with the major movements of the time, and at the time I was homeless between 1986 and 1991 this seemed to reach a culminating moment. Not only was there a lot of interest in the Cold War, but my personal life seemed also to be tied into the political events of the time. I was convinced that my political experience and knowledge went beyond books, the TV or the media. At the same time, I was undergoing a personal transformation that meant my everyday reality was inextricably bound with politics and history.

My teens had been spent in the Sixties, when full employment and the satisfaction of material needs were taken for granted. I lived a comfortable life as a schoolboy and everything seemed just to be a matter of doing what you liked best, for all your needs would always be provided. At school I learned how this was done, studying Keynesian economics. I could follow the major events of the time including Budgets and devaluation, sure in their logic and certain that the macroeconomic sums were working out all right. My personal welfare coincided with the heyday of the welfare state.

Then in the mid-70's things went wrong and I couldn't understand it. All that I had learned and taken for granted at school and university no longer worked. There was inflation and unemployment at the same time, something I had been taught was impossible, and the economy was ruined. At the same time I was taken into psychiatric hospital. My fortunes plummeted. I lost my freedom. I had to share wards and dormitories with other mental patients. I could not choose my food. I lost my car. As I was on in-patient benefits I was grindingly poor. As the country went into ruin, so my own fortunes also took a downward turn. Then in the early Eighties the byword became capitalism. It became the current mode to get a good job, get a house and progress with the free market under Margaret Thatcher. This coincided with me moving to London, working in the City, getting credit cards, owning my own house and car. I moved with the spirit of Thatcherism.

Then I was made redundant and lost my house in the High Court on 1st April 1986. I stayed with the spirit of the free market and spent all my money and credit on travel to Europe as much as I could, but when I became homeless and destitute, it appeared that I had duly suffered my comeuppance and then the reality of capitalism hit me. Because I could no longer buy a good lifestyle, I had to rely on State Agencies which were unable to pick me and tens of thousands of others up. With the rhetoric about the Cold War from Ronald Reagan and Star Wars supported by Margaret Thatcher, it became apparent to me that I must be involved as a major actor on the Soviet side, having been naturally rejected from that alien mode, capitalism.

From Keynesian full employment and assured

futures, to economic breakdown, to having money and buying things, to the end crisis of the Cold War, my fortunes seemed to lead me naturally to identify with the times. Not family, work, sport or any other story. I seemed to fit in with the large social and political factors that I lived with. And this was the underlying belief and perception which was how I thought during five years of schizophrenic homelessness.

In a strange way, the past seven years have also been a coincidence between the social and the personal, but I don't have that sense of identity with the changes of society due to the fact that my schizophrenia is controlled by suitable medication. My last release from hospital in 1991 coincided with Care in the Community, and I have led a dignified, supported but independent life since then with no more crises and hospital admissions.

Andrew Voyce

Privateering

The effect of my experiences led me to believe
that I was a soldier who had a duty to follow what
he had learned of world affairs and to place his
loyalty accordingly. Not only that, but I was to be
self-supporting in the cause. As I say elsewhere in
this booklet, my life appeared to mimic some
aspect of politics and economics at various
junctures. I had at various times helped to create
some measures of wealth in my working life. I had
been given a certain proportion of that wealth, and
it was for my self-determination to decide how I
applied that which I had. It is a fact of life, known
to political theorists as alienation, that there is no
direct link between what we produce, how
valuable that product is, and what our nominal
status is, and what we actually receive at the end
of the day. As I say, what I ended up with was to
be spent as a demonstration of what I was. It was
not a result of any process that could in any way
be described as fair, just, or as an advertisement
for others to follow what I had done. Quite the
opposite in most cases. Nevertheless, I was
usually in possession of some financial resources,
be it only £4.77 per day homeless dole rate, and it
was for me to use those resources, small or large,
in the cause or causes that I knew to be right.
Such as preparing the way to some small extent
for the incoming Soviets. At various points, I may
not have had money, but I did have time, and it
was my duty to use that time, together with my
small but real resources, to purposes that I, as an
educated adult over the age of 21, knew to be

right and just. Coincidentally, I came to believe, there was also another transaction in my life that did reflect the value I had added to the process in a precise and real way. That extra value, I thought, had not come to me in a fair and equitable amount, but had actually been put aside to fund that which I now needed to support my lifestyle. I believed that this creamed-off funding had not gone to my various rip-off employers which included my own family, but had fortunately been requisitioned by the state, and was now existing in the form of a Treasury Bill issued every month or so. Part of that Treasury Bill went to pay my £4.77 a day dole money, but the rest of the asset value I had helped to create had been seized by the Treasury and was used to pay for the traffic that accompanied me everywhere I went, and for useful devices such as hypnotic tricks which were used to help me in this hostile world. Such magic might include the tricks used to keep me from freezing to death in the winter, as I slept out in parks and in bus shelters. In my attempts to unravel this system and pay it complimentary heed, I attempted to decipher my dole Giros. I sought patterns in the numbers and graphics on the Girocheques and would try to remember them after I had cashed them in case I could find them again somewhere else, or if they might contain some signal that would tell me what to do or where to head for. It all had meaning. Nevertheless, I still did have some choices about how to spend my dole, or other resources as they became, unfortunately rarely, available. Before I became destitute when I had a period in custody which destroyed my DHSS claim, I was not so badly off, and could make larger choices. I was made redundant in late 1985 after, I'm afraid, psychiatric symptoms appeared at work. I am not saying that I was due for the chop, because my firm was taken over and the new owners were putting in their own men. But in the time immediately prior to the takeover, the therapeutic effects of my medication had completely ceased. This was because I would not take any more medication by injection, and no alternative, although readily available, was offered. So I simply stopped turning up for injections once I was away from a care situation where I lived, in this case a Richmond Fellowship house in Putney. I had escaped that situation by buying a house in one of the poorest parts of London once my salary could afford the mortgage. But in due course, as had happened at other times when I had escaped injections, paranoia and delusions began to take over. There were beginning to be one or two incidents, warning signs really, and they happened at work. So I think that when the new owners were looking round for suitable old firm employees to sack, I would have had no-one to speak up for me. Not that it need have been that bad. I could have taken the £4000 redundancy cheque and bought a new car and used my work record, which now spread back for four years, to negotiate perhaps a better job elsewhere in the City. But schizophrenia doesn't work like that. I read somewhere that the average length of mortgage arrears in the UK at the time was over 2 years. So I could afford to take the dole cheque that in those days included mortgage payments from week one, and sit around for two years at least. Without meeting the arrears on the loan. In fact, the efficient American bank I had the loan with had got the possession order from the High Court all done and sealed within five months. That was a surprise for me! Nevertheless, I had this inflated dole cheque as long as they held off getting an eviction order, and I also had the £4000 redundancy, and credit cards. There was even some profit in the value of the house which could also be mine, but I didn't actually get that for several years, when the bank sold the house with vacant possession for a knock-down amount, and then I had to get a solicitor to get the money out of them, which was not easy because by then I was on the road, homeless.

So with these various resources, I decided to try and make more, and eventually to spend most of it in my new career of privateer, rather like a 17th century seaman might have done. The first thing I needed to do was to practice arms. As I had found several times before, I couldn't get either a firearms or a shotgun licence, even though by now I was a householder, due to police objections, no doubt owing to my minor criminal record and official history of mental illness. I had some acquaintances who had illegal firearms, but the ownership was not really the point. It was the combination of ownership and officially approved firearms certificate status that I wanted. No, rather than engage with my dubious friends, I became aware of what you could do abroad. There were

TV programs on Beirut and the Afghan refugee camps in Pakistan. With the four- way war in the Lebanon, taking part was a matter of personal commitment. I saw a programe about an area of Beirut where there was this luxury lifestyle, with sun and sand etc. And by the swimming pool was a local arms dealer. All you had to do was get a plane out to Beirut, whose airport was incredibly still working, find this swimming pool, buy whatever gun you liked and then make your way to the war zone where you could fire away and see if you could kill someone. The Afghan deal was similar. At first after I lost my job, I still considered myself to have allegiance to the Americans, for my firm, both old and new, was American, and they after all paid the bills. So I considered it also to be a good thing to consider going to the refugee camps in Pakistan where, according to the TV, you could buy a rifle for $200. It was then a simple matter of walking across the border into Afghanistan with a group similarly armed, and you could have a go at the Russians. With my resources, I could well consider these options.

I became increasingly aware of things around my house that I hadn't previously noticed because I had been away at work during the day. What I became concerned about was the incredible traffic noise. It was non-stop. I tried to analyse it and concluded that the pattern of traffic noise was a series of crescendos. There might be a prominent noise of diesels, say busses or lorries, followed by a prominent noise of small noisy motorcycles, and so on . The pattern never ceased, it merely modulated. Once I had realised that there were these patterns, I acted to get rid of one of the most noisy, namely diesel dustcarts that always shook the streets of terraced houses they came so close to when collecting. As there was no noticeable connection to government to get action that I knew of, I decided that the locals and the people who monitored financial accounts and who could make, for example, bank errors in your favour, would have to do it themselves. So I set up a building society account called The Plumstead Voluntary Association for the Reinstatement of Horsedrawn Dustcarts. Once enough money had been paid in through donations and favourable bank errors from right-minded officials, we could then purchase horses and carts and put them on the council depot up the road, like the Young's Shire horses that pulled drays in the City. It was just a matter of getting the right sum and then we could succeed. I considered it a done deal. At first, after my redundancy, I also became involved with music. I had just finished an Open University course in Popular Culture so I thought I knew what I was doing. I got myself an electric guitar and amplifier with a twin tape deck so that you could overdub tracks and one instrument could sound like a whole band. I recorded several tracks, both old and newly composed. One track was the first tune I ever learned, Wipeout. I thought this was great, and would be a hit. I also thought that several other tracks would be hits in Europe, in Holland and Germany. I thought I would soon be coming into a few hundred thousand in various currencies. However, a group called The Fat Boys with Fun Boy Three went to number one with their version of Wipeout. This added to the paranoia I was feeling. I thought that the hit record was directly connected to what I was doing. I thought that, as with previous rip-offs from work I had done, this was another rip-off. However, I then began to realise that the surplus from the record sales would be added to the value of the Treasury Bill that was generated in my name, as with the value I had created but not been paid for in full, for example by labouring on my parents' building sites from the age of eleven. I made this realisation about the time that I became rejected by America, when I was refused a visa for a quick visit to New York. The reason the American Embassy gave was that there was some doubt that I owned my house. I felt insulted and would not demean myself to appeal. If that was the way they wanted it, so be it. I began to look for meaning in financial instruments like my Girocheques and elsewhere and gradually began to think that the Soviets were taking a part in my finances by taking part of the Bill in my name. That led to an interest in signalling in general.

The other main time when I was in funds was in about 1989, two or three years after I lost my house. I was staying at Sittingbourne Spike, a homeless institution of the DHSS, when I managed to persuade a local solicitor to obtain the surplus from the sale of my house by the bank. This was the sale price less debts approved by the court, which were the mortgage, arrears, and credit card debts. (To add to my delusion that this was a military situation, the solicitor had the title of Major. Whether in the TA, retired, drum major or what I don't know). The cheque I got was for just over £13,000. This sum starting with the number 13 immediately said to me: unlucky. A kind of joke message. I looked at the other figures in the sums, and tried to find a signalled meaning. What could that cheque have meant? Perhaps a new top-of the-range car, new clothes, some left in the bank for a rainy day, and the impetus to get a job. I knew that I probably would not get credit, certainly not another mortgage, but still, I could probably manage to rent a decent place if I got it together.

But as when I was in funds after the redundancy, schizophrenia played its part. By the time I got the change from the sale of the house, I had gone several years without medication, and I was really deluded (but did not either suffer the debilitating effects of injections, which were for me much worse than the symptoms of the illness). So, in that state, what did the £13,000 bring me? What I did was to spend it over a year or so, travelling around my home area of the South-East, taking photographs and buying Chinese meals. I put the money in the Post Office and drew out £20-£50 a day. I did not claim the dole any more. I did buy some good trainers and several cameras, as well as some good waterproof clothes. I did not get in anywhere, and as often happened, got evicted from the Spike to go out into the wilds. I believed that I had a duty to pay for anything where there was a lack of obvious funds. Usually this meant that when I went into a rural church service and there were few parishioners and the plate looked empty, I would put ten or twenty quid in to cover that day's heat and light for an hour. Once, I witnessed an accident in Sittingbourne where a motorcycle knocked over a young woman who lay prostrate in the street. I put her in the recovery position and covered her with my coat and supported her head on my pullover. Then the ambulance arrived and took her to hospital. That day I bought her some supplies and took them to the hospital, but as they said she had been discharged, I left the food and drink for someone else. I felt it was my duty to take care of everything as I was the one with funds. I then went to the ambulance station in the evening when it was closed and put three twenty pound notes through the letterbox, as I thought that would be about what the journey and depreciation on their vehicle etc would cost. As I had instigated the rescue and not walked away, I had to pay.

I was also able to buy things like paint and brushes for Morse code signs which I painted at the dead of night in woods. I could buy tools and equipment as much as I needed to help the Soviets, from B&Q and places. But generally, if you're going to travel around the South-East by train and bus or taxi, take photographs of the area which can be reconnaissance for your future comrades, which the developer will let your distant unknown friends have, and get copies of your photos by one-hour processing so you can leave them around for your bin-man-cum-spy to find, you are actually going to need about £13,000 over a year or so. When I was poor and on day-rate dole, I would buy the occasional Stanley knife to cut down blackberry bushes near country paths to prevent enemy insurgents living off them, or perhaps I would buy an indelible pen to mark up traffic counts on lampposts, again for friendly incoming Soviets to find to tell them what to expect. When I was in the Spike, I would buy, out of my weekly £9.84, when it finally came through, a reward for the staff if they had got rid of someone I didn't like, such as someone from another part of the country. That would usually be a quarter of tea, but if they had expelled someone from Yorkshire, the reward would clearly have to be a Yorkie bar. They would get the connection. Also in Sittingbourne, they used to close the main drag for traffic-free shopping on a Saturday. I would wait early in the morning for the council men to come and lower the barriers, and would be delighted to give them their reward as a sign of approval, this usually being a can of Coke.

I considered the value I had contributed to economic enterprises to be quite large, for I happened to have been involved in enterprises where there was a considerable social value, not to mention profit. I noticed in 1989 that a house I had helped to build in Sevenoaks was for sale in a local estate agent for £200,000. It was the firm's policy to build detached houses for the upper end of the market, because there was always someone willing to buy expensive property. I had been involved with that set of people, with mostly my family in charge, from the age of eleven to twenty four. It included some years digging ditches with my artificial leg. The total number of these luxury dwellings was several dozen. If you take what I had physically done, there was a good proportion of the roof insulation; I had unloaded a certain amount of the bricks by hand in the days before pallets; I had mixed concrete for a certain number of drives; I had unloaded some of the total of roof tiles and timber; I had painted a certain amount of timber, wall and fencing; I had done the office work of paying wages and suppliers for some time; and as a primary schoolboy I had suggested the name of the original firm. It was not everything, but it was not nothing. It had a value. There was, finally, the appearance I gave to the firm as a unified family business, something that bankers took notice of in those days when assessing whether to give loan finance. For all that, the most I was ever paid was seven pounds a week. I never had one of those houses for myself, and indeed only ever had succeeded to be occupier with a mortgage of a terraced house in the poorest part of London. I spent years as a homeless wanderer. As I have said previously, the technical social scientist's term for this is alienation, where there is no link between what you do and where you get your sustenance from, and this process usually involves exploitation. Many people see things like home ownership as a panacea, a be all and end all. In fact, homes are mere commodities that are built and traded in a market merry-go-round where any semblance of permanence is purely illusion. But I came to believe that this was the same as other one-sided employment deals. Such as when I spent a year doing the books of a Tunbridge Wells insurance broker. When I joined him, he was trading on borrowed time. With my experience of what his creditor insurance underwriters would accept as excuses for later payment, I extended his borrowed time by a whole month, thus creating a big plus in the bank account. We used that as deposit on a freehold building in the town centre, and virtually immediately made a considerable paper profit. This made the firm solvent, saving the owner and his other employees. However, I was not paid enough even to afford a mortgage on the cheapest place in town. I did however, enjoy the intellectual challenge of that year. So, there was, I believed, a considerable amount to my credit in the Treasury Bill that I was associated with. Mainly, it went to pay for the traffic which kept me isolated but safe. It was a fact that even in 1987 there were hardly any parts of the South-East where there was no traffic. It ran night and day. I tried traffic analysis all night on several occasions, and recorded lorries, cars and motorbikes right through, twenty-four-seven. My traffic was paid for by my Treasury Bill, with at times a mere £4.77 coming to me each day. However, as the Soviets took a share of the Bill, so I was given some useful powers. Nominally, I learned to wear many layers to survive the winters out. What actually happened was that at night I would be put to sleep and taken by magic to a warm place and then returned in the morning. I was given protection so that my artificial leg lasted for several years and I became able to walk long distances by taking regular breaks. If I needed to wake up in the middle of the night to do some signal painting, I could do so without an alarm. This too was supernatural intervention from Siberia. I became convinced that it was this that enabled me to survive. I believed that I too might become an ancient being along with those I already knew. These included Jesus, who was merely 2000 years old, Norman Knight who remained with us from the days of William the Conquerer, and the Ancient Marines who were from the time of Elizabeth 1, and who I had met in full uniform in an ice-cream bar in Folkestone.

All this came to an end when I was arrested whilst trying to break into a hut at Oakwood psychiatric hospital in the middle of one night. The grounds happened to be swarming with police. I was not charged, but was put into the hospital under section of the mental health laws. I managed to escape being put onto injections after some forceful negotiations. Shortly afterwards, the Eastern Bloc collapsed. I have not been in hospital or on the road since.

The Islamic Republic of Iran

Like many others, I had had some knowledge of Islam since my schooldays, which were in the fifties and sixties. I knew that they worshipped Mohammed, who they did not regard as we regard Jesus, as the son of God. But Mohammed was so important that they were sometimes called Mohammedans. I knew they went on pilgrimages to Mecca where they walked around a holy object seven times. I knew they did not drink alcohol, and prayed five times a day facing Mecca. I also knew they could have five wives, and that they cut off the hands of thieves, one for the first offence, and the remaining one for the second offence. I knew that during one month, the month of Ramadan, nothing was supposed to pass their lips between dawn and dusk. This I had learned at school really as a by-product of history lessons, where we had been filled in with some details about Moslems during the Crusades. Also from the sixties, I remembered how Cassius Clay had become a Muslim and changed his name to Muhammad Ali, and was aware of the Black Muslims of America who were led by Malcolm X. At some point I became aware that Muslims believed it was sinful to make images of living souls, and that photographs could destroy the Muslim's religious integrity. Also their artwork, be it carpets or painting or mosaic or whatever, always contained a deliberate mistake, for only Allah was perfect. There was also something about Arab Muslims only eating with the left hand, as the right was reserved for something dirty. When I was involved

Andrew Voyce

with the student fringe drug-taking scene in the
early 70's, certain things about Islam became
implied. One of my associates had made the
overland journey to the East in the previous year,
and Muslim countries were associated with drugs.
We were primarily concerned with hashish in all its
forms, resin, herbal (marijuana), and liquid
(occasionally talked of). Some Muslim countries
were associated with hard drugs that we
considered to be un-cool. Not least because being
caught by the authorities with hard drugs in those
places meant a firing squad. The hottest places
were on the way East, Turkey and the Shah's Iran
(and also Singapore). The film 'Midnight Express'
featured hash smuggling in Turkey. It was known
that you would not be shot for possession or
smuggling of hash in Turkey or Iran, but you could
look forward to many years in some very
unpleasant jails if caught. Nevertheless, the
unwary in those places, such as in 'Midnight
Express', were often the victims of police spies
and entrapment. But once past Iran, you were into
Afghanistan, and the good times began. There
seemed to be the suggestion that in Muslim
places friendly to hippies where hash was openly
available, it was their form of alcohol. This
extended from Afghanistan with its main towns of
Herat, Kandahar, and Kabul, over the Khyber
Pass into Pakistan, into Kashmir with its
houseboats, and into more multicultural ethnic
places in India, Goa, and Nepal. Right through this
part of the trip you would be stoned with local
approval. About the main risks were Delhi belly,
and having your home-bound parcels ripped off by

the postal staff for the stamps, meaning no arrival of fresh supplies via the mail when you got home. Hash seemed to be a way to mystic experiences started in the East and copied by Western kids on a journey. It was implied that Muslims used hash to reach God, or a higher plane, as well as for other purposes such as the Assassins, a name derived from 'hashish'.

Whilst occupying houses for the purpose of all-day hash smoking, eating or drinking, in the student fringes in Reading, I read a book called 'The Lost Centuries' by Sir Arthur Glubb. It was a chronicle of life in the East from the times of the Mongol Hoards onwards. One incident involving Genghis Khan stood in my memory for a long time, and I will refer to it again later. The Golden Hoard had many and spectacular ways of dealing with their enemies. If outriding emissaries failed to secure the surrender of a city, the Mongols would be merciless. If the town or city had a moat, the Mongols would sometimes drive assembled prisoners into the ditch, especially if it contained hazards such as blades or stakes. They would then march over the dead bodies and scale the walls. No mercy would be shown to any place that did not give in when it had the chance. Another way the Mongols had of taking a city was to divert whole rivers so the walls would be swept away, before, as before, slaughtering the inhabitants. On one occasion they diverted a river that flowed 500 miles into a Central Asian lake, I believe it was the Aral Sea, so that it then flowed 500 miles in the opposite direction into another lake, I believe the

Caspian Sea. The re-direction remains on our maps today. A mere trifle to affect modern geography, in the cause of taking a town. However, it was in fact the Muslims of the Middle East who stopped the Mongols. There were, in Egypt and elsewhere, slave dynasties headed by Sultans including Saladin. They were a military race from near and far. They were known as Mamluks, and indeed the last king of Egypt, Farook, who was deposed in the 1950's, was of the Mamluk dynasty. The Mamluks beat Genghis at a battle called Jal-al-Din, led by a warrior named Baybers. So if it were not for the Muslim civilisation that stopped Genghis in the 13th century, we in Europe might now be Mongols. Amongst the warriors of the Mamluk kingdoms were the Assassins, who would do evil deeds for their Emir and Sultan masters. Traditionally, they were supposed to be high on hash whilst committing political murders and other foul deeds. It seemed fitting that during this time in Reading, whilst reading of these times gone by in foreign places, that I managed to buy two half pound bags of Lebanese hash, one of Gold and one of Red. The bags had neat images of Arab boys on them, reinforcing the link we assumed existed between some Muslims and the mysticism of cannabis, which probably went back to The Lost Centuries of Glubb.

In the early to mid 80's, I became more acquainted with Islam whilst living in Plumstead in south-east London and working in the City. When the old lady living next door to me died, a family of foreign origin moved in. I talked briefly to the oldish male of the house across the back wall, and he told me that he had been saved from madness by reading and remembering two lines of the Koran. His English was not that good, and I didn't have many more conversations with him. I thought perhaps he had some connection with Muslim areas where there were, at the time, conflicts. These were in Afghanistan, where they were fighting the Soviets, and there was also a war of Muslim against Muslim, between Iran and Iraq. At work for an American insurance group, we got to handle the group's worldwide claims in the court set up in The Hague to deal with the settlement of businesses between Iran, a newly declared Islamic Republic, and the United States, following the hostage crisis of 1979-80. My boss actually went to The Hague and we kept in touch by phone, and I would supply him with whatever figures he needed. At times it was very acrimonious, and a judge in the tribunal was once physically attacked by an Iranian lawyer. It was really the beginning of militant Islamic fundamentalism. About this time, which coincided with my last days in the City, I became aware that some people just above my level were not only being paid for the 9 to 5 job, they were also doing private deals. It appeared from what I knew, that some people with knowledge were facilitating settlements where they were close to the action or knew players, in return for a commission. When I had been made redundant, and later was refused the visa for a trip to the States, I became anti-American. I beamed up, with a torch, a signal to

Andrew Voyce

Ronald Reagan's spy satellite in (incorrect) Morse Code, challenging him to drop the Bomb on us incompetents in London. When the Bomb was not dropped, I decided I must help the Iranians at the Iran-America Tribunal in The Hague, as we had a mutual enemy in the USA. I knew that the insurance company in the City had some small doubts about our status and contractual ability, but of course we had not told the Iranians. I decided that this would be valuable information, and could be an excuse for the Iranians reneging on their agreement with my former employers, and that this would save the Iranians several hundred thousand dollars. To be absolutely sure, I went by boat and train to The Hague and asked a taxi driver if he knew where the Iranian delegation had their headquarters. He knew, and took me there, waiting whilst I delivered my letter containing my information. The deed done, I returned to the station and came back to England. In the letter, I said that I realised that there might be some commission, but that it may be difficult to pay me direct, so could the Islamic Republic please put any credit to the name of the children of the Muslim living next door to me in Plumstead, for their benefit. A few weeks later, the Islamic Republic wrote to me, but sent the letter by mistake, not to me at No 6, but to me at No7, the house next door. On the envelope it quite clearly had 'The Islamic Republic of Iran'. When my neighbour brought the letter to me, he looked somewhat pale and shocked. To think that I had communications with the fundamentalists of Ayatolla Khomeni. The letter thanked me for my information, but mentioned nothing about any commission. I considered it a job done.

This kind of gelled some ideas about how you went about modern day conflicts. There would be a lot of autonomous action, and self-sufficiency. Sometimes you might get pay from a source such as the commission on doing the dirty on the Iran-America tribunal, but quite often you would have to make do as best as you could, and a corollary of that would be that you should be generous and help like-minded people if you could. What good was money if you couldn't use it in the cause? At first, after I became redundant, I had resources. These were, to use the current phrase, non-renewable. That didn't bother me. I thought that something would turn up, not considering that that something might be homeless destitution. I had finances at the time, and that was all that I knew. So, on my frequent jaunts around Europe, there were some moments that consumed a lot of resources. Extravagant is not the right word for this, because I was not setting out to have a good time and do some conspicuous consumption; rather, I was setting out to support the cause, whatever that was. One jaunt took me from an airport in Germany to Istanbul. I had vague thoughts that perhaps there was some possibility of re-diverting the river that Genghis Khan had caused to flow from one Central Asian lake to another a thousand miles distant (I have mentioned this above). This, I thought, could be done by driving convoys of those brightly-painted lorries you see in pictures of the East, through the supply tunnel the Russians had built to keep in touch with their forces in Afghanistan, into Central Asia, and then to drive the lorries, maybe laden with cement, into the watercourse in question, and to divert the river back to where it flowed before Genghis came along. This would be a sort of sporting gesture of combat to the Soviets. I had thoughts of somehow financing these convoys of trucks from somewhere like Istanbul, and indeed in Istanbul, I saw some brightly-painted lorries.

However, before I could start approaching the truck owners, I had a misfortune. I hired a car and went round Istanbul, entering what I thought must be Asia. At an area called Taxxim, I got out of the car and hired...a taxi. I asked the driver with his local knowledge to take me to a nightclub. He did this, and I discovered that the services of the hostess who kept ordering drinks in the club totalled $1100. The bill was presented by a group of particularly vicious men. Luckily, I had the money in travellers cheques in my pocket and escaped without being knifed or murdered. Then... I couldn't find the hire car again. So I headed for the airport where, by fortunate coincidence, a Lufthansa flight was ready for take off, back to Germany. Then back to England by train and ferry. So I put the whole episode, nightclub fleecing, lost car and all, behind me.

That was about the last episode I had with Islam for some time, although I did go to Regent's Park mosque to try to get some update on my trip to The Hague, strangely enough without success, as the Imams knew nothing of it. There then followed a very unsettled period in which I did indeed discover that my resources were finite. I spent several years destitute, until I got the change from the sale of my repossessed house. For some time I only had contact with local people and those I presumed were either American or Soviets, and did not feel the presence of Islam. I used some of that money from the house sale to make a trip to Perth in Scotland by overnight coach, for that was the original base of the Stagecoach company which was taking over many bus companies in the South. On the coach, two men boarded who I immediately took an interest in. They were both very well built and of Eastern origin, but they sat apart as if they did not know each other, and my suspicions were aroused. I somehow made a connection between my previous thought paradigm about re-diverting the river in Central Asia and these men. Like I was for some of the time, they were of independent means and were connected to this idea of getting through the tunnel from Afghanistan to Uzbekistan to drive trucks into the river, but it had to be done when there was a window to get through the tunnel. I imagined great waves of combatants circling either the Soviet or Western spheres and then suddenly heading for the combat zone hoping to steal an advantage and gain the objective. But they always clashed and the focal point, the narrow tunnel, was always jammed. While they were not actually in the combat zone, men like these on the coach would have to avoid booby traps and snipers who could be anywhere. Near the end of the journey, as dawn broke, we were leaving the town of Hamilton when it appeared that some cars followed us. I considered this to be connected to the two combatants, who got off in Scotland, and who would soon be making tracks to the combat zone that I had been thwarted from reaching by the fleecing in Istanbul.

Part of me became linked in my mind to issues perceived around Islam. That part was my amputated leg. I had had strange wonderings about the thing. What had actually happened under anaesthetic? Had there been a chance of saving the leg in 1968 (as I believe there now would be following experience in Northern Ireland and other places of armed conflict)? Had this chance not been taken because I had been judged by the surgeons to be unworthy of an able-bodied adulthood? Had this judgement been subliminally implanted by some recording in my mind when they made those final cuts? With hindsight, I am sure that there were those I met along the way, particularly those suffering mental doubts and torments, who might have been affected by meeting an amputee. In over thirty years since the loss, I have only seldom heard comments such as 'onelegged man' or 'peg-leg', and rarely to my face. However, if I can have weird imaginations, I am sure other disturbed people too would have found the proximity of such severe trauma difficult to cope with. Some may have thought, perhaps: I hope I'm not next. Who knows? My experiences of asylum life included meeting Muslims in numbers for the first time in my life in England. I had met some previously, in Kenya, and I had been worried by a remark made to me, that putting your elbow on the open window ledge of a car could get it stuck off by another car. There were associations with double amputation, the penalty for thieving twice. Having been convicted of theft (of petrol) before being sent to an asylum, there were thoughts in my mind concerning the Muslim psychiatrists and nurses, and the punishment they might have thought suitable for theft: another amputation. Or was the one already existing a downpayment sufficient to cover the crime? Were some of them guilty of crimes that would merit amputation, and was I an uncomfortable reminder? When I went to Istanbul, before I went to the nightclub where I was fleeced, I went around the city in shorts, showing off my leg- the first and only time I have done that. I felt there were many issues this raised. There were those concerning theft which I had experienced in NHS mental hospitals, but there was also the fact that many of the people I met would have died had they suffered my trauma in Turkey, for they would have had no insurance to pay for the operation. In a way, I had been privileged. I am sure that my selective knowledge of the Islamic world made my thoughts on their community and how their world worked, a lot less coherent. It is perhaps the area where my delusions were connected most to misapprehensions and ignorance, but that is how I interpreted Islam and its people, and it has to come under the heading of psychotic delusory syndrome.

Andrew Voyce

Survival

I did not really get the knack of survival in the open until the mid-80's, but I had been on the road several times before. I believe the police term is wandering abroad. I had suffered badly at the hands of the NHS regimes in the mental hospitals where I had been detained, sometimes by the devious and dubious means of probation orders with psychiatric conditions. This meant that, unlike detention under Section of a mental health act, I had no appeal. They insisted on giving me a mixture of tranquilliser and sedative by injection every two or three weeks, despite my objections. This would leave me in a very unpleasant condition of restlessness and tiredness, totally debilitated. This would last for a week or so, followed by a few days feeling not so bad, and then it would start all over again with another injection, called a depot. There was, along with this, no alternative to the hospital support system. There was nowhere else to get a bed apart from the ward dormitory, and nowhere else to get food but from the ward dining room (at the times set down, or not at all). If you smoked, as most people did, you were given meagre wages in the hospital Industrial Therapy unit, and a small amount of DHSS pocket money, which also had to buy you clothes, soap, razor blades, or if you were female, tampons. You had very little or no choice. The whole system was heavily unionised, with the BMA for the doctors, and NUPE and COHSE for the other staff. This system was known as corporatism by social scientists, and it meant that there was never ever the sack for anyone, no matter what they did or how they behaved. Fortunately, Margaret Thatcher smashed the unions and closed the old asylums, otherwise I am sure I would have spent much more time in those places, being injected and forced to work in the IT units, for administrative ease. As it is, I have so far spent a decade without injections or in-patient time, after the passing if the Community Care Act. Thank you Margaret.

In order to escape the NHS regimes before the Community Care Act, I would have to be 'rehabilitated' from the hospital to some extension of the NHS, such as local authority hostel or Pentecostal church hostel with its own IT unit. I could usually find some menial work at these locations in towns, but the purpose of the care situation was to continue the injections. Eventually, I would escape, sometimes after getting a car. For some reason, it usually occurred in the winter. Thus, I needed shelter. What that usually meant was living in my car, driving around to get the heater to work, and then running short of money. I would then exist by filling up the car and driving off without paying, and stealing milk from doorsteps. Sooner or later I would get arrested. I had escaped the injections, but the result was that delusions and paranoia from having no therapy, would return. The circumstances of my arrests often added to my paranoia. The police really can muster four cars and a van to stop and arrest a petrol thief. It felt like the crime of the century. The police never asked me why I had done it. They simply returned me, sometimes after a court appearance, to psychiatric care, where the injections would start again. I went through this revolving door procedure several times over the last years of the 70's and into the 80's.

One, if not the main, feature of buying my own house in one of the poorest parts of London in the mid-80's was to escape from a hostel and hence the obligation to have injections. After a while I became deluded and paranoid, for I need therapeutic medication, but not in the form of injections, which I will do anything to avoid. Once I had become homeless and destitute after losing my job and house, I managed to maintain myself without committing my previous petty crimes. I learned to survive a winter or two out in the wilds. I left London when I had become homeless, because you are always disturbed during the night, usually by the police. This I considered could be dangerous, and you could get attacked; indeed as I now have found out, you are many more times likely to die a violent death as a homeless person, than if you live in a house. I returned to the county town of the area I most called home, Kent. I was fortunate to have my DHSS claim dealt with swiftly. I got £4.77 a day. This enabled me to go to the supermarket and buy things like individual pork pies and cheese and milk. Without that dole claim, I would have been in dire straights, for there were no organised soup kitchens in Maidstone in those years. I slept out of town. I think that was a crucial move, for town is

Andrew Voyce

where the danger is. Out of town, there are bus shelters and places like the dry area under evergreen trees, which are safe. No-one will ever find you to attack you there. In Maidstone also there were the open summer houses at the psychiatric hospital, Oakwood (now closed). I tried to observe precautions like moving to the night area after dark, and lighting cigarettes under cover at night in case anyone sees you. In about five years, I was found by the security at Oakwood only once. They were pretty rough considering I did not resist them, but I did use my camera to protect myself and confuse them. They called the police, who took me to the police station and then left me at the hospital, but I managed to get the nurses to let me go, and returned to sleep out. I was often tempted to break into the Occupational Therapy huts at Oakwood, and when I did I found the heating was on all night and I could make a cup of tea. It was a temptation I tried to avoid for it might lead to attention falling on me. It was eventually my downfall, for in attempting to break in again one night, I found the whole gardens was infested with police, who arrested me and then got two doctors to put me in the wards at Oakwood under section of the 1983 Mental Health Act. I was able to appeal that time, and negotiated to avoid the administration of injections. I was put on a more suitable form of medication to which I did not object, and have not been re-admitted since.

There were two main things to cope with whilst destitute: the cold winters and lack of cash. When I was on a daily rate of £4.77 dole, there were rules that went with it. Tuesday to Thursday was straightforward- you got a Giro of £4.77 at 3.3Opm which you then cashed. On Fridays, however, you got nothing for the weekend, only that day's pay. So you had £4.77 to last Friday, Saturday and Sunday. Believe me that was hard. I felt hunger. I had learned to pick up dog ends and roll them up at the spike in Sittingbourne. That was the only way I could support my addiction to cigarettes. For food over those weekends, I sometimes was left with half a packet of biscuits to last all Sunday and Monday until I got the Giro at 3.30. That was a good Giro, to include the weekend before. It came to £13.31. But although it sounded a lot, I never managed to save any for the next weekend, and the starvation would happen again. The rhetoric of the time is expressed in a phrase of the draconian 1986 Social Security Act :- 'requirements less resources'. It was assumed that if you cut benefits back to below living standards, people would still find something. They might have something to sell, like a stereo or walkman or car or something. Some have to sell their bodies. Or they might find a friend who will help them. That's the resource you use to meet your requirements. Unfortunately, for some people, like for example kids with no education, coming out of, say, an abusive care home, at the age of 16 or 17, the 1986 Act does not actually provide for any right to benefit for them at all (only discretionary) and benefits are savagely reduced until the age of 25. For them too, there is only a limited right to the minimum wage, and before New Labour reinstated it, there was not even that if they got work. As I found out, the 1986 Act can mean starvation, right into the 21st century. As for the cold, I learned to survive the winters without the luxury of a car with a heater. I found that moving around helped a lot in the cold. You just had to force yourself to keep going. I had found out what it was like to endure a night of cold before I had become destitute. While returning from Europe one November, I decided to see what would happen if you had no passport. So I put it on a train at Vlissingen station that then went on its journey to Amsterdam. I then decided further to see what it would be like if I missed the ferry. So I watched it leave at 11pm and went into the port building for warmth. Only to be evicted by the staff who were closing the place until the next morning's sailing. Dressed as I was in only an unlined bomber jacket, I stayed in the light all night, so that the security men could see me from their booth (for safety). Every ten or fifteen minutes, I would do some vigorous exercise to warm up. Come the next morning, the security men gave me a coffee and allowed me back into the terminal. There I went through a procedure making some kind of declaration to enable me to get a paper to go through customs and return to Sheerness. So I had found out what it would be like to spend a frosty night outside and also what to do if you lose your passport. It was a bit like requirements less resources. In Maidstone I did keep moving at the worst, coldest times. I also found that it was not only necessary to find a safe place to sleep, but that you need plenty of layers to survive. You can actually get a reasonable night's sleep. You need to arrange you clothes over you so you are cocooned beneath your layers which should be properly arranged over you. At all costs avoid getting wet. Sleep on plastic bin liners to prevent the damp finding you. For the winter climate of mid-Kent, which typically has three or four weeks of snow in winter, I had the following : a T-shirt, then a pullover, then a body warmer which I got right inside at night, then a lined bomber jacket, then a wax jacket with hood which kept all the damp out. I found things like tents and sleeping bags just made it more difficult to get around during the day, and didn't really make that much difference at night. You are permanently cold in such conditions, but you can survive, and even a few degrees of warmth such as when you go into a shop or mall really makes the day. Gloves are also essential- I used to prefer the fingers cut off for dexterity. When the spring comes, you really appreciate it, and by then you know you can survive the worst.

I had one set of experiences where I was sure that the magician, who took me away at night to keep me from freezing to death, was picking my pockets too. By this time I was allowed to sign on weekly, and got a lump sum of £75 every fortnight. It allowed me freedom to roam from Maidstone. I also remember that my 40th birthday was a signing-on day. The post office that cashed the Giros always gave me a fifty. On one occasion, I decided to visit Sevenoaks to do some traffic counts on lampposts. After one night in my favourite spot under a tarpaulin over some bales of horses' hay, I discovered that the magician had stolen my fifty pound note. That left me less than twenty to last until the next Giro day in almost a fortnight's time. I was distraught and desperate. I went to the police station, for they were responsible for lost property, and I knew that they knew about the lost note. When all they could do was report the loss of a fifty pound note, I got serious. It would appear that I, as a glorified signaller and would-be political commissar, would have to do some serious infantry fighting. I kept on referring to some locals I knew, and to termination, repeatedly, assuming that he knew that I was saying that I would have to break in there, and would kill if necessary. I assumed that he knew I was carrying a Stanley knife as well as the indelible pen for traffic counting on lampposts. I left to carry out the deed. It was do or die. I laid low close to the house I knew of until it was the small hours. I then approached the house and made sure my knife was at hand. I knew there was a shotgun inside. The windows were best Everest double glazing, sound and shatter proof etc. It took a large garden ornament, which I unleashed under the covering sound of a passing HGV, to break in. Instead of the anticipated confrontation, there was no-one there to challenge me. I looked in the office and found a fifty pound note and credit cards. I was saved. I made off and headed for the nearby village of Kemsing, which had a youth hostel. I left the credit cards at the youth hostel for foreign, presumably Soviet, tourists to find. That night was a Saturday, and I slept in the porch of the church. When I awoke the next morning, the damn magician had done it again. The second fifty quid note had gone from my pockets. Some trained SAS and Royal Marine Commando men know how to make nettle tea and which mushrooms to eat, and can survive quite well in the English countryside. Not me. I needed money to buy food in supermarkets and now I was broke again with still a long way to go to the next Giro. Requirements less resources. I had my back against the wall that Sunday morning. In desperation, I went to church and explained my predicament to the vicar who passed me on to one of his parishioners. That gentleman was good enough to give me twenty quid. A lifesaver. I walked back to Maidstone over the next ten days or so, living really frugally and smoking dog ends. When I got my next Giro, I went back to the church in Kemsing and repaid the kind parishioner with thanks. I managed to budget to pay off the twenty and survive to the next payday, but that was the only time when I lost any cash over the years, and it happened twice in one go. Apart from the victimless crime of breaking into the NHS OT hut at Oakwood, that break in at Sevenoaks was the only time I did any deliberate crime for gain, and I considered it an infantry action, which could have turned out either win or lose.

Elsewhere, in prisons or police cells or spikes, you needed different tactics to survive. The dangers are different. They mainly concern violent attack, either from fellow inmates or the staff. Sometimes you have to put up with virtually inedible food, in places like F Block in Brixton Prison, known quaintly as Fraggle Rock. Probably because of the

Muppets there. You never know what goes into the grey liquid of porridge, and as for the beef curry... You just have to put up with that. But some times you can really feel like a combatant on the job. I was repeatedly kept on remand over about three months for an eventual sentence of a conditional discharge. After each weekly remand hearing before the beak at Horseferry Road in London, we would all go to Lambeth Holding Centre where we would be grouped for dispersal to various police cells across the South-East. It could be anywhere: Great Yarmouth, Milton Keynes, Kent, the New Forest, anywhere. But you got really good treatment on these jaunts. You got free fags from the police guards at regular intervals, good grub from the police canteens, regular cups of tea through the cell opening, and an exiting coach ride at either end all handcuffed up and with a police escort. These journeys could take place at any hour of the day or night. There were drinks and biscuits on these journeys to and from court, and I thought I was being introduced to safe places within the British state that could be used by any dignitary, including, one day, perhaps me again. I thought each police cells had its own code, decipherable from the grid on the bottle glass windows, hence 5 up by 3 across would give the code 53. Easy, isn't it? I thought I was being taught something. They were indeed safe places, and I didn't know the hurricane of 1987 had occurred, because I was in cells and the outside simply can't be felt. I was attacked by inmates once or twice, but wasn't hurt and the sort of things I had learnt at all-boys school and on building sites were good. It never pays to make yourself noticed by anyone, and when you say something it had to be in the right idiom, to express the usual sort of prejudices and things that don't obviously go against your cellmate if you have one. Call the screws 'sir' and they will leave you alone. It's really common sense. Don't stand out from the crowd. When I had days in cells on my own, I would do things like climb up the walls spread between my outstretched hands and feet. I never fell. I would sometimes set myself tasks, like 200 press-ups between breakfast and lunch, or to spend all day with my arms above my shoulders, with a ten minute break each hour.

There are other things that can make all the difference. They concern health. For some reason, when I was destitute and homeless, I thought it would be OK to use mouthwash alone to take care of my teeth. I think that was because I didn't want to mess up my pockets with toothpaste and wet toothbrush. But I found out - mouthwash alone does not work. When I was in Sittingboume spike, passing the office as I went out, I felt a slight hammering on my gum. I assumed that the DHSS staff had developed a pain gun. I left the spike soon after, but the pain followed me around and got worse. I blamed it on this pain gun that was following me and rattling my teeth. I eventually got to Maidstone and decided to ask a dentist about the pain. I managed to find one straight away, who extracted a black molar. I had had an abscess. However, I continued with the mouthwash, and again suffered the consequences. One Christmas, the United Reformed church in Maidstone opened up a shelter. However, on the Christmas Eve I bought a very sticky gummed sweet, which completely dislodged a bullet of a filling. That Christmas dinner would have been my first hot meal for a year, but the pain of any food or drink that was hot or which played on my sore, gaping tooth, prevented me from eating until I went to an emergency dentist the day after Boxing Day, to have the tooth removed. By then, the Christmas shelter had closed, so I had to wait again for that first hot meal. Care of teeth is important when you are on the road, but often neglected, as I found to my cost. There was one healthcare item which I was very lucky with. That was my artificial leg. During this time, I got quite fit, and did repeated short distances, sometimes carrying a rucksack full of photographs, with plenty of breaks. In this way, I could overcome my disability and cover quite long distances in quite quick time. You might see me sitting down somewhere along a footpath, and maybe later somewhere else, without realising that I was steadily eating up the distance on my way. However, such abuse of a prosthesis is really destined for disaster. I was lucky that I could tolerate all sorts of pro-temp alternatives to officially supplied stump socks, such as ordinary foot socks which I was given by prison officers. Sometimes, on the road, I would bandage my stump in the fashion I had learned when first in hospital. I would leave the bandages, when bloody and used, strung across footpaths where I had spent the night or rested. To be ready for action, I slept with my prosthesis on. Only on one occasion did I suffer mechanical failure, and fortunately I was in Sittingbourne spike when it happened, so I did not have to move around very much. The foot completely broke off, and luckily after a few days of having it tied on with a bandage, they got me to the Limb Fitting Centre at nearby Gillingham, where a new foot was attached. I don't think many people can expect to get that amount of hard wear out of an artificial leg, and indeed I thought that this was probably due to a magician/mesmerist, courtesy of the secret NHS, who repaired my limb for me without my knowing, as I went along.

There was only one other time when I was as desperate as when I had lost those two fifty pound notes. The second big crisis involved my health. As well as being permanently cold in the winter, I often had a runny nose. I got used to this, but during one winter I developed flu. I found that I could no longer bear the low temperatures one night, and was suffering uncontrollable shivering. I had to do something or possibly develop pneumonia. There didn't seem any possibility of getting into a warm hospital ward, so I decided reluctantly to get myself put into a cell. Once I had decided what to do, I went ahead. I took some paint I had and threw it at a psychiatric group home I knew nearby. I then phoned the police and told them what I had done. A short time later, several patrol cars arrived. They took me back to the vandalised house and got me to clean the paint off. Then I was driven, not to a warm cell, but to a village outside Maidstone town limits, and left there. It was the middle of the night. I assumed that was a signal to do what I needed to do, and broke into the village hall. I wrapped myself in a curtain and got some rest. The cleaner found me next morning and called the police. At last I was taken before a magistrate and spent the next month recovering from the flu in Canterbury Jail. I was released on time after the worst of the winter was over, and did not get pneumonia.

There were some unique moments. These included waking up in the middle of a winter night and seeing the moon light up the clouds, with the lit-up ground gleaming with frost. Or, getting started at dawn in mid-summer, in broad daylight at 4.30 am, with the birds singing and no-one around on foot for hours. I recall the sense of security being under my covers in a bus shelter as a violent storm lashed down all around, in darkness with the roar of the wind, but safe and dry. These were experiences that do not come your way in ordinary lifestyles. However I did not experience these events as such, expecting them to result in, amongst other delusions, the dawning of a Soviet invasion, communications with ancient beings, or signals to parallel universes.

www.ingramcontent.com/pod-product-compliance
Lightning Source LLC
Chambersburg PA
CBHW031220290326
41931CB00035B/600